The Curious
CAT

The Curious
CAT

Contributing Editor
FERN COLLINS

CHARTWELL
BOOKS

Quarto is the authority on a wide range of topics.

Quarto educates, entertains and enriches the lives of our readers—enthusiasts and lovers of hands-on living.

www.quartoknows.com

This edition published in 2016 by
CHARTWELL BOOKS
an imprint of Book Sales
a division of Quarto Publishing Group USA Inc.
142 West 36th Street, 4th Floor
New York, NY 10018
USA

ISBN-13: 978-0-7858-3476-2

10 9 8 7 6 5 4 3 2 1

Printed in China

For all editorial enquiries, please contact:
www.regencyhousepublishing.com

Images used under license from
©Shutterstock.com

The Owl and the Pussy-Cat

Edward Lear (1812–1888)

The Owl and the Pussy-Cat went to sea
  In a beautiful pea-green boat,
They took some honey, and plenty of money,
  Wrapped up in a five-pound note.
The Owl looked up to the stars above,
  And sang to a small guitar,
'O lovely Pussy! O Pussy, my love,
  What a beautiful Pussy you are,
    You are,
    You are!
What a beautiful Pussy you are!"

Pussy said to the Owl, "You elegant fowl!
  How charmingly sweet you sing!
O let us be married! too long we have tarried:
  But what shall we do for a ring?"
They sailed away, for a year and a day,
  To the land where the Bong-Tree grows
And there in a wood a Piggy-wig stood
  With a ring at the end of his nose,
    His nose,
    His nose,
  With a ring at the end of his nose.

"Dear Pig, are you willing to sell for one shilling
  Your ring?" Said the Piggy, "I will."
So they took it away, and were married next day
  By the Turkey who lives on the hill.
They dined on mince, and slices of quince,
  Which they ate with a runcible spoon;

And hand in hand, on the edge of the sand,
  They danced by the light of the moon,
    The moon,
    The moon,
They danced by the light of the moon.

CONTENTS

INTRODUCTION

Cats have been domesticated since prehistoric times, perhaps for as long as 5,000 years. Throughout human history, they have been greatly valued as destroyers of vermin, as well as for their ornamental qualities. However, considering our long and successful relationship with the domestic feline, the phenomenon of the pure-bred cat is a surprisingly recent one.

How many breeds of cats could you identify? The chances are that you might recognize at least a few of the following: Persian, Maine Coon, Siamese, Abyssinian, Russian Blue, Tonkinese, Burmese. These are, in fact, just a few of the 40 or so breeds recognized by the world's major cat registries. There are a handful more that are quite new or rare and not yet officially recognized by many feline associations.

Cats have graced us with their presence since the time of the ancient Egyptians, possibly much earlier. But it took the rise in popularity of cat shows in late 19th-century England to kick-start the selective breeding of the domestic cat into separate types. All but a few domestic cat breeds are less than 100 years old, and most of them appeared on the scene far more recently. Compare this to the dog world, where rudimentary selective breeding started several thousand years ago.

OPPOSITE: Cats have been used for catching mice and rats since ancient times.

The Maine Coon is an instantly recognizable breed.

A TIGER IN THE HOME

The domestic cat is related to lions, tigers, pumas, and other wild cats and the similarity in looks and behavior is immediately apparent. However, it is the smaller wildcat which is the cat's closest relative. The Scottish Wildcat is a fine example and its superb natural camouflage enables it to merge imperceptibly into the surrounding countryside. It is adaptable, hardy, and extremely timid. Further south lives the Jungle Cat which, despite its name, inhabits the sandy desert regions of Egypt and has a beautifully ticked coat which blends in splendidly with the surrounding terrain. There are many other wildcats in evidence throughout the world, but due to extreme timidity, little is unfortunately known about them. In fact, wildcats appear in many places, in the snow-enveloped north, in deserts and mountains and in every case have managed to evolve to fit their environments. These adaptations have filtered through to our domestic breeds: for example, the Russian Blue is an inhabitant of the Baltic region of Europe, where the climate is predominately cold, so it fortunately came equipped with a dense, luxurious 'double coat' to keep it warm. Likewise the Angora and Persians of upland Turkey and Iran also have thick coats valuable for keeping the cold at bay during the bitter continental nights. At the other extreme, the Oriental breeds have paler, silkier, and thinner coats, to reflect the heat of the tropics, and which keep them correspondingly cooler.

Feral cats live in organized groups, usually in the vicinity of human populations where they can either scavenge for food or rely on food provided for them by local people. The Colosseum in Rome has such a colony where people bring them food and their way of life has changed very little for centuries. Other groups such as Egyptian bazaar cats have an ancient lineage and are to this day highly respected by the local people.

The Siberian Tiger is related to the domestic cat.

PAGE 13: Cats and humans have held a strong relationship lasting thousands of years.

THE DOMESTICATION OF THE CAT

Remains of cats have been found from the pre-pottery Neolithic period of Jericho (circa 7000BC), though these may have been hunted animals or the equivalent of modern feral cats, attracted to food scraps, and at best tolerated. However, tamed cats have possibly lived in association with humans far earlier than archaeological and historical records imply. Cat remains (bones, teeth) are often retrieved from prehistoric sites, but it is impossible to know whether these were companions, or prey killed for their pelts and meat. Later, instead of hunting them, humans would have deliberately encouraged the presence of cats as rat catchers.

The ancient Egyptian domestic cat, which spread to Europe in historic times, was used as a retriever in hunting as well as for catching rats and mice. It was probably derived from *Felis lybica* or one of the other North African wildcats. The modern domestic cat is probably descended from this animal, perhaps with an admixture of other wildcat species, or of species domesticated at various times in other parts of the world. Once the Egyptians had given up the nomadic lifestyle and learned to till the soil, they settled into agrarian communities. Since these communities depended for their very existence upon their crops, which could only be harvested

once or twice a year, a means of storing them between harvests had to be found. Early on, this consisted merely of keeping grain in baskets. This attracted mice, rats, and other vermin, which attracted the local lesser cat, the African Wildcat. People started encouraging the cats to stay close by to catch the vermin by leaving out scraps. Since they had a ready source of food, no threat from the people, and an absence of enemies, cats moved in on a permanent basis. Being a naturally calm species, the African Wildcat quickly adapted to people, allowing itself first to be approached, then petted, and eventually to be held. People began to appreciate the cat's other qualities: its nocturnal habits meant it hunted round the

OPPOSITE: An African Wildcat.

A statue of the Egyptian cat goddess Bastet.

clock and, unlike the dog, it was a clean animal that buried its waste outside, away from its den.

In ancient Egypt, cats were not only established as domesticated animals, but were even cherished and worshipped as gods and religious idols. This was due to their status, in this agrarian society, as rat and mouse catchers. So cherished were they, that to kill a cat, even accidentally, was an offense punishable by death. If a house-cat died, the owners shaved off their eyebrows as a sign of mourning.

Numerous cat mummies have been found; many appear to have been sacrifices and cats would have been reared in large numbers for this purpose. Paintings would seem to suggest that cats were used in the hunting of wildfowl, although this is debatable since cats are not generally good retrievers. Later, they were depicted in paintings as symbols of fertility and/or domestic harmony.

Although Ancient Egyptians forbade the export of cats, by 1700BC the cat was being depicted in domestic scenes in the Holy Land. By 1400BC domestic cats were present in Greece. By 1000BC cats had traveled northwards across the Mediterranean aboard ships (possibly with Phoenician traders) and from there they spread along trade routes. The cat traveled eastward to China and Japan (where it protected silkworm cocoons from rats). In Japan, cats were so highly valued that they were not allowed out of the house, even when a plague of rodents threatened to devastate crops.

The Romans regarded cats as rare and exotic pets, preferring the mongoose for vermin control. By 500BC, domestic cats seem to have been familiar in southern Europe. The cat may have arrived in England with the Phoenicians who traded for tin in Cornwall, though it is most likely that it was the Romans who first brought cats with them some time before AD4. Further cats arrived with the Vikings.

During the early Middle Ages, the Norse goddess Freya was the closest thing to a cat goddess among the Europeans. She was constantly surrounded by cats and her worship contained many cat-oriented rituals. When Christians barred her worship, Freya became a demon and the cat became a manifestation of the devil. Cats became associated with witches and were even believed to be able to change form from cats to witches and back at will. Thus, being a symbol of Satan, cats were burned, killed and buried alive, walled up in brick buildings, thrown off towers, and tortured as part of religious rituals to drive out the devil.

The cat's popularity subsequently grew again, both on land and sea, because of its expertise in rodent control. Cats traveled alongside man in ships, valued as protectors of ships' supplies, and as lucky mascots.

There was a very long period before the cat embarked on its voyage to the New World in any numbers. Although cats were taken to Quebec in the 1500s, and at least one cat accompanied the Pilgrim Fathers to America in 1620, it was not until the 1700s that domestic cats traveled to America with colonists and began to establish themselves on this continent. The cat penetrated Australia with Europeans in 1788, though aboriginal histories indicate that cats were already present on parts of the Australian coast as shipwreck survivors. There is no indigenous species of feline in Australia.

Folklore surrounding black cats has varied from culture to culture.

OPPOSITE: The ship's cat has been a common feature since ancient times.

THE CAT

William Henry Davies (1871-1940)

Within that porch, across the way,
I see two naked eyes this night;
Two eyes that neither shut nor blink,
Searching my face with a green light.

But cats to me are strange, so strange -
I cannot sleep if one is near;
And though I'm sure I see those eyes,
I'm not so sure a body's there!

THE CAT AND THE MOON

William Butler Yeats (1865-1939)

And the moon spun round like a top,
And the nearest kin of the moon,
The creeping cat, looked up.
Black Minnaloushe stared at the moon,
For, wander and wail as he would,
The pure cold light in the sky
Troubled his animal blood.
Minnaloushe runs in the grass
Lifting his delicate feet.
Do you dance, Minnaloushe, do you dance?
When two close kindred meet.
What better than call a dance?
Maybe the moon may learn,
Tired of that courtly fashion,
A new dance turn.
Minnaloushe creeps through the grass
From moonlit place to place,
The sacred moon overhead
Has taken a new phase.
Does Minnaloushe know that his pupils

Will pass from change to change,
And that from round to crescent,
From crescent to round they range?
Minnaloushe creeps through the grass
Alone, important and wise,
And lifts to the changing moon
His changing eyes.

LONGHAIR GROUP

The true longhaired cat is the Persian, also sometimes known as the Longhair. The breed is probably descended from matings between Angora cats, which originated from the Ankara region of Turkey, with others from Persia (now Iran). It is said that the first examples of these longhaired cats reached Italy and France in the 16th century. It wasn't until the middle of the 19th century that the cats acquired pedigree status. Persians are now bred in a staggering array of colors and patterns.

The typical Persian cat has a luxuriously silky coat that consists of long guard hairs and shorter down hairs. Unfortunately, because of the nature of their coats, even the most fastidious self-grooming Longhair will still need daily grooming by its owner. If you are considering owning a Longhair, the time taken for such regular grooming must be taken into consideration, as well as the fact that being year-round molters, your carpets, clothes and furniture are likely to be liberally coated with cat's hairs, too. However, there is no denying the unbeatable opulence – and placid, friendly nature – of the Persian cat.

PERSIAN

The ancestors of the Persian Longhair (known as Persian in the USA) were stocky, longhaired gray cats imported from Persia into Italy in the 17th century, and silken-haired white Angora cats from Turkey that arrived in France at about the same time. In the late 1800s, the Persian was developed in the UK with the black being the first to be accorded a formal breeding standard. The original stocky build is still an essential mark of today's Longhair breed, although other characteristics have been dramatically altered. By the beginning of the 1900s, the breed had been recognized by all registries.

The body is massive and powerful, with a short neck, a broad chest, and short, stocky legs. The paws are large and round,

A Cream Persian.

and may be tufted. The head is big and round, with small, round-tipped ears, and a short, broad nose. The eyes are large, round, and set wide apart. The tail is short but very full to match the luxurious coat.

The Longhair has a full and flowing coat of long, dense fur that tangles easily and needs daily brushing and combing to prevent matting. The fur around the neck is extra long, forming the typical ruff.

Quiet and affectionate, but somewhat detached, the Longhair is ideally suited to living in an apartment, as it prefers to be indoors, but may also enjoy outdoor life. It is the breed most likely to accept other cats into its home. These cats are gentle by nature, and as kittens are playful and mischievous.

WHITE

The result of matings between the earliest imported Angora and Persian cats. The original, blue-eyed variety was prone to deafness, so it was cross-bred with Blue

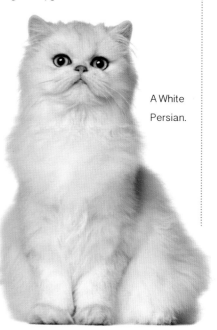

A White Persian.

and Black Persians. Some of these offspring had blue eyes, but some had copper-colored eyes, and others had one orange or copper eye and one blue eye. These odd-eyed Whites are likely to be deaf on the blue-eyed side of the face. In some cases White Persians are judged as three separate varieties, according to eye color.

A Black Persian.

OPPOSITE: A close up of a Red.

BLACK

The earliest Persian breed to have been officially recognized; today, however, it is quite rare.

The glossy, raven-black coat is prone to developing rusty tinges, thought to be caused by strong sunlight or damp conditions. To maintain the coat, therefore, the cat needs to be kept in cool, dry conditions free from direct light. Periods of molting may also cause brownish bars to appear on the coat.

A Cream kitten.

RED

Until quite recently, the Red Persian was one of the rarest of all feline varieties. This was largely because of the need to select parents that had displayed few if any tabby markings as kittens, combined with long fur and intensity of color which is deep, rich, clear, brilliant and red coat without markings, shadings or ticking.

CREAM

The Cream Persian is a dilute Red, with probable input from the white Angoras that were cross-bred with Persians in the 1880s. At first, cream cats were often discarded by exhibitors in favor of cats with stronger coat colors. In the early 20th century, Creams were eventually imported into the USA from the UK and soon established themselves as successful show winners. Faint tabby markings usually disappear as kittens mature. Other colors include Blue-cream and Lilac-cream.

CHOCOLATE

The Chocolate Persian derives from the mating of a Chocolate Point Siamese with a Blue Persian. Through generations of breeding, however, the Chocolate has established itself as a variety in its own right.

LILAC

Another offshoot from the breeding program for Colorpoint Longhairs was the Lilac Persian. These cats have some Siamese in them, which may account for their independent, yet affectionate, natures.

BI-COLOR

At first, longhaired cats with patches of white were disqualified from shows, but eventually, these 'magpies' or bi-colors were allowed to compete and eventually new standards were drawn up by cat associations globally.

PERSIAN VAN BI-COLOR

Any solid color with white. Color distribution is different from that of the Bi-color, being a white cat with the color confined to head, legs and tail.

A Bi-color Persian.

PEWTER

A relatively recent development is the breeding from Tortie Cameos which produces kittens with black rather than red, cream, or tortoiseshell tipping.

SMOKE

Black Smokes were the first of this color to be bred. At first they were considered to be rather poorer versions of the Blue Persian, and as such were kept as domestic companions rather than as show cats. At a UK cat show in 1893, the Smoke Persian was given its own breed class and enjoyed a certain popularity for a time at the beginning of the 20th century. However, since then the breed has declined and is

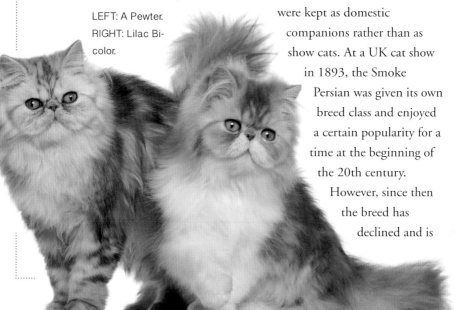

LEFT: A Pewter.
RIGHT: Lilac Bi-color.

nowadays a rarity. In the USA, however, the story has been different, where it has always found favor and has begun, more recently, to be bred in other colors than black.

Smoke colors include: Black, Blue, Red, Lilac, Chocolate, Tortoiseshell, Blue-cream, Chocolate Tortoiseshell, and Lilac-cream.

CAMEO

This color was first bred in the USA during the 1950s. There are three varieties of shading in Cameos, which take a while to develop. These are Shell, Shaded, and Smoke. Due to their exceptionally friendly nature and their particularly unusual coat-coloring, these cats have become immensely popular worldwide.

A Black Smoke.
OPPOSITE: A Red Shell Cameo kitten.

TABBY

Tabby colors include: Silver, Red, Brown, Blue, Cream, Cameo, Silver Tortie, Brown Tortie, and Blue Tortie.

TORTOISESHELL

It was not until the beginning of the 20th century that tortoiseshell Persians first made

A Brown Tabby.

appearance at cat shows. They have become extremely popular, not only because their docile nature makes them ideal as pets, but also because of the intriguing fact that all variations of tortoiseshell are usually female. This occurs because of the complexity of their genetic inheritance.

Colors are Tortoiseshell-and-White and Chocolate Tortoiseshell.

A Tortoiseshell-and-White.

CALICO (USA)

Colors of the body are white with unbrindled patches of black and red. White is predominant on the underparts. Eye color is brilliant copper. There is also a Dilute Calico.

CHINCHILLA

The Chinchilla dates back to the late 19th century in the UK, and occurred as the result of an accidental mating between a female Silver Tabby and a male cat of another color. By the beginning of the 20th century these cats were being imported from the UK into the USA and have continued to gain popularity in both countries.

Colors are Shaded Silver, Shaded Golden, and Golden.

OPPOSITE: A Dilute Calico.
A Shaded Silver Chinchilla.

COLORPOINT LONGHAIR

(Himalayan)

Experiments in crossing a Longhair and a Siamese began in the early 20th century. The result was the Colorpoint Longhair – cats of the typical longhair, Persian type but with deeper color restricted to the cat's 'points.' These are the extremities: the face (or mask), the ears, legs, paws, and tail. The breed had been accepted in the UK and the USA during the 1950s and by the 1960s, the breed was recognized worldwide.

A Chocolate Point.

The Colorpoint is of medium to large build and stocky. The head is round and massive and the eyes large, full, and round. The ears are small and round-tipped. The paws are large, round, and firm and the tail is short but in proportion.

OPPOSITE: A Seal Point.

The coat is thick, dense, and glossy with no trace of woolliness. There is a full frill over the shoulders, continuing between the front legs. Thorough daily grooming is required to keep the coat in good condition, paying particular attention to the underparts between the hind and fore legs, under the tail, and around the neck.

Colors include: Solid Point in Seal, Blue, Chocolate, Lilac, Red, Cream, Tortie, and Blue-Cream. Tabby Point in Seal, Blue, Chocolate, and Lilac.

As one might expect, the Colorpoint has inherited some of the best traits of its ancestry. These cats tend to be more lively than the typical placid Persian but not as noisy as a Siamese. They are calm and friendly and make relaxed but outgoing companions.

OPPOSITE: A Cream Point.
A Lilac Point.

JAVANESE

There is a lot of confusion surrounding the use of this name in the cat world, although it is always used to describe cats of distinctly Oriental type. It has been adopted simply because of the tradition which has grown up for using the names of countries and islands from south-eastern Asia for other Oriental breeds, such as the Siamese and Balinese. Unfortunately, it has been used to describe different cats in the past, rather than being applied to a particular breed. The longhaired form of the Oriental is now perhaps best-known under this description, having been bred from crosses between Orientals and longhairs of Oriental type. But some US cat organizations adopted this description for the non-traditional varieties of the Balinese, notably the red, tortie, and tabby varieties of this pointed breed rather than solid-colored Longhaired Orientals. As a result, the description of Javanese may be applied both to solid and colorpointed cats, depending on the show classification.

The Javanese, as a Longhaired Oriental, has a wedge-shaped head and medium-sized, almond-shaped eyes. The ears are large and pointed and the

A Red Tabby Javanese.

body is long, svelte, well-muscled but dainty, with the shoulders no wider than the hips. The cat has long, fine legs ending in small, dainty, oval paws. The tail is very long and thin and tapers to a point, with the hair spread out like a plume.

The coat is fine and silky, medium-long on the body and without an undercoat. There is a frill round the shoulders and chest. Regular gentle brushing keeps the coat in good condition.

Colors, as for the Oriental Shorthair, include: Black, Blue, Chocolate, Lilac, Red, Cream, Cinnamon, Fawn, Tortoiseshell (all colors), Smoke (all colors), Tabby (all colors), Tabby-tortoiseshell, or Torbie (all colors). The eye color for all color varieties is a vivid, intense green or blue.

Active, always alert, and very inquisitive, the Javanese has an extrovert personality and is intelligent and quite vocal. It is a very affectionate cat and loves human company. It hates to be left alone for long periods.

"No matter how much cats fight, there always seems to be plenty of kittens."— Abraham Lincoln (1809-1865)

THE CAT OF THE HOUSE

Ford Madox Ford (1873-1939)

Over the hearth with my 'minishing eyes I muse; until after
the last coal dies.
Every tunnel of the mouse,
every channel of the cricket,
I have smelt,
I have felt
the secret shifting of the mouldered rafter,
and heard
every bird in the thicket.
I see
you
Nightingale up in the tree!
I, born of a race of strange things,
of deserts, great temples, great kings,
in the hot sands where the nightingale never sings!

SEMI-LONGHAIR GROUP

Some breeds of longhaired cats are more accurately referred to as semi-longhairs. The distinctive feature that sets semi-longhairs apart from true longhairs is the length of their underfur. This is significantly shorter than that of their guard hairs, whereas in Longhairs, they are of similar length. As a result, the longer fur of the semi-longhair lies flatter, particularly when the coat becomes thinner in the warmer months of the year, accounting for their resemblance to shorthaired cats at this stage. Coat care is more easily achieved in semi-longhairs, compared to genuine Longhairs because it is less dense, lies flatter, and is less easily matted. Regular grooming is required, but at nothing like the level of that required of a true Longhair. Semi-longhairs, therefore, are a good choice of cat for the pet owner who enjoys the look of the Longhair, but not the hard work of constant brushing. Many semi-longhair breeds, such as the Maine Coon, owe their long fur to their ancestral habitat and the necessity to develop protective 'clothing' in harsh environments. However, others, such as the Balinese, are newer breeds, developed purely because of the aesthetic pleasure of their luxurious coats.

BALINESE

Once known as the Longhair Siamese, the Balinese is a silky, longer-haired version of the Siamese cat. The cat's gracefulness and lithe build are reminiscent of the temple dancers of the Indonesian island of Bali, in whose honor the breed is named. The long-coated kittens that sometimes appear in litters of Siamese cats were developed into the Balinese in the USA in the 1950s. The new breed was introduced to the UK and Europe in the 1970s.

The Balinese is of medium build, but long-limbed and lithe. It has a long, wedge-shaped head, wide between the ears and narrowing to the nose, which is long and straight. The cat's most distinctive feature is its almond-shaped, slanted sapphire blue eyes. The ears are large and pointed, and the tail is very long and thin, with hair spread out like a plume.

Since it has no undercoat, the Balinese's long and typically pale-colored fine top coat feels exceptionally silky and lies flat to the body. The colorpoint fur can be in a range of colors and patterns. The coat needs regular gentle combing, while the tail should be brushed.

Colors include: Solid Point in Seal, Blue, Chocolate, Lilac, Red, Cream, and Apricot. Tortie Point in Seal, Blue, Chocolate, Lilac, Cinnamon, Caramel, and Fawn. Tabby Point in Seal, Blue, Chocolate, Lilac, Red, Cream, Seal, Blue, Chocolate, and Lilac.

Not surprisingly, Balinese are similar in temperament to the Siamese. They love to be the center of attention and want to be part of the family, amusing people with their acrobatic antics. They are usually affectionate but can be aloof. Although they are a little quieter than their Siamese cousins, their voices are penetrating nonetheless.

OPPOSITE: A Cream Point Balinese.
A Tabby Point.

BIRMAN

First bred as a pedigree in France in the early 1920s, the beautiful semi-longhaired Birman was slower to gain popularity in the USA and the UK, where it was not recognized until the late 1960s. Various legends attempt to explain the ancestry of the Birman as originating from the temples of Burma (now Myanmar). However, the true origins of the breed are unknown.

The Birman's large body has thickset legs of medium length and short paws that end in distinctive white gloves. The head is broad and rounded, with full cheeks and a strong chin. Eyes are almost round and deep blue. The tail is medium-length and full.

The coat is long, silky, and slightly curled on the belly, with a full ruff around the neck. All Birmans are colorpointed, with darker coloration on the ears, face, tail and legs.

A Tabby Point.

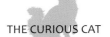

A Lilac Point.

The coat is comparatively easy to keep well-groomed with regular brushing and combing.

Colors include: Solid Point in Seal, Blue, Lilac, Red, and Cream. Tortoiseshell and Tabby Point in Seal Tortie, Blue Tortie, Chocolate Tortie, Lilac Tortie, Seal Tabby, Blue Tabby, Chocolate Tabby, Lilac Tabby, Red Tabby, Cream Tabby, Seal Tortie Tabby, Blue Tortie Tabby, Chocolate Tortie Tabby, and Lilac Tortie Tabby.

Birmans are proud, intelligent, and inquisitive. They love people and are extremely loyal. Birman kittens are particularly mischievous and their sense of fun stays with them into adulthood. They are also gentle and sensitive, and being sociable animals, will tolerate other cats and dogs quite happily. They quickly adapt to new surroundings, but have a tendency to pine if left alone for long periods of time.

A Seal Point.
OPPOSITE: A Lilac Tabby Point.

MAINE COON

This is one of the oldest natural breeds in North America and has been recognized as a true variety for well over 100 years. The breed originated in the state of Maine on the north-eastern side of the USA. The name 'coon' arose because it was once thought that the cat was the product of matings between domestic cats and racoons – although this is not biologically possible. A more romantic theory suggests that Marie Antoinette sent her cats to America during the time of the French Revolution, and these became the ancestors of the breed. The more likely explanation is that the Maine Coon resulted from matings between local domestic cats and longhaired cats introduced by sailors

A Silver Tabby.

visiting coastal towns. A Maine Coon won the Best in Show award at the 1895 Madison Square Garden Show, but the breed did not achieve wide international recognition until the 1980s. In fact, it faded from the cat scene in its homeland in the early 1900s, as breeders preferred to show more exotic cats, such as Persian Longhairs, which were introduced to the USA from Europe at this stage.

Four Maine Coon kittens in assorted colors.

A handsome, sturdy, medium to large cat. The head has a gently concave outline when viewed in profile, with a squared-off muzzle. The nose is of medium length. Eyes are large and slightly oval, and the colors may range from green, blue and hazel to copper. The large ears are wide at the base and set well apart on the head. The tips of the ears bear small tufts of fur. The Maine Coon has a long, muscular and-well proportioned body with medium-length legs and large, round paws. The impressive tail should be nearly as long as the body.

These are semi-longhaired cats with heavy, shaggy fur. It tends to be thicker and longer around the back, sides, and belly, but there

A Red Tabby.

should also be a full frill around the neck, although this is lost when much of the longer hair is molted in the spring, being a feature associated with the winter coat. The fur on the tail should be long and flowing. Many colors are recognized in the breed; tabby patterns are common.

Colors include: Solid and Parti-colored in White, Black, Blue, Red, Cream, Tortoiseshell, Tortoiseshell-and-white, Blue-cream, Blue-cream-and-white, and Bi-color. Smoke and shaded in Shaded Silver, Shaded Red, Black Smoke, Blue Smoke, Red Smoke, and Cream Smoke. Tabby in Silver, Brown, Red, Blue, Cream, Cameo, Tortie (or Torbie), Tabby-and-white, and Tortie Tabbie-and-white.

A Tabby-and-white.

Although large, these cats are sweet-natured, friendly animals. Both attractive and amusing in their antics, they are considered by many to be the ideal pet cat. They are slow to mature and may take up to four years to attain full adult stature.

"When I play with my cat, how do I know that she is not passing time with me rather than I with her?"

Michel de Montaigne
(1533-1592)

OPPOSITE and BELOW:
Tabby-and-White Maine
Coons.

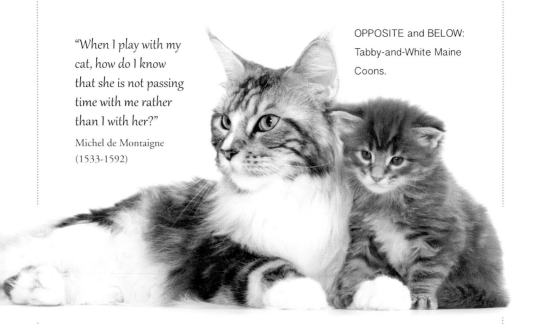

NORWEGIAN FOREST CAT

Though its origins are unknown, it is possible that the Norwegian Forest Cat can trace its ancestry back to longhaired Turkish cats, which had arrived in Norway by around AD1000 with Viking traders from the East. For centuries, the 'Wegie' was used as a working cat on Scandinavian farms. It was not until the 1930s that it was taken seriously as a breed, and planned breeding did not begin until the 1970s. The first Wegies arrived in the USA in 1979 and in Britain in the 1980s, since when the breed has established a strong international following.

Its long, strongly built body, and long hind legs give the Wegie a solid bearing. The cat's head is triangular with a long, straight profile, and the ears are pointed and erect. The eyes are large

A Silver Tabby-and-white.
OPPOSITE: A Tortoiseshell-and-white.

and open and the chin is firm. The tail is long and bushy and the paws are tufted.

The Wegie's double-layered coat grows heavier during winter to keep out both cold and wet. A woolly undercoat keeps the body warm, while a smooth, water-repellent upper coat keeps out rain and snow. The generous frill of fur at the neck and chest is likely to be shed during the summer months.

Colors include: Solid in White, Black, Blue, Red, and Cream. Tabby in Silver, Brown, Blue, Red, Cream, and Tabby-and-white. Parti-Colored in Tortoiseshell, Tortoiseshell-and-white, Blue-cream, Blue-cream-and-white, and Bi-color. Cameo and Smoke varieties in Chinchilla, Shaded Silver, Red Shell Cameo, Red Shaded Cameo, Black Smoke, Blue Smoke, and Red Smoke.

A Brown Tabby.
OPPOSITE: A Silver Tabby.

The Wegie is generally alert and active. It can be very playful while retaining the independent character of its semi-wild forbearers. It is affectionate but dislikes being cosseted and will defend its territory vigorously. It is a superb climber and hunter, and has even been known to fish in streams! This cat must not be confined indoors.

In Norwegian Forest Cats, there is no relationship between the coat color and eye color, as found in most other pedigree breeds.

A Brown Tabby.

"The smallest feline is a masterpiece."

Leonardo da Vinci (1452-1519)

Three "Wegie" kittens.

RAGDOLL

The world's largest domestic cat, the Ragdoll is a relatively new breed. Originating in California, the first steps towards creating it were rather muddled. A mitted Seal Point Birman male was mated with a non-pedigree longhaired white female. The resulting semi-longhaired kittens were cross-bred to produce the first pedigree Ragdolls. The first breeder coined the name Ragdoll because of the cat's tendency to go limp in people's arms. The Ragdoll has become a firm favorite in the USA and has been exported to Europe and Australasia.

A Blue Bi-color.
OPPOSITE: A Lilac Point kitten.

The Ragdoll has a large build, with a medium to large head. The full cheeks taper to a well developed muzzle. The ears are medium-sized with rounded tips. The eyes are large and oval. The Ragdoll has a long, muscular body, medium legs, and large, round paws. The tail is long and bushy.

The Ragdoll's coat is semi-long, shorter around the head and longer

Ragdoll kittens in assorted colors.

OPPOSITE: A Lilac Point.

towards the tail. The soft, silky texture makes it less prone to matting than the fur of many longhairs, and needs only moderate grooming. The coat is dark compared with other pointed breeds.

In all varieties the body is light in color and only slightly shaded. The points (except the paws and chin) should be clearly defined, matched for color, and in harmony with the body color.

Colors include: Mitted – The chin must be white and a white stripe on the nose is preferred. White mittens on the front legs and back paws should be entirely white to the knees and hocks. A white stripe extends from the bib to the underside between the front legs to the base of the tail. Seal Point in Blue, Chocolate, and Lilac.

Bi-Color in Seal, Blue, Chocolate, Tabby, and Lilac. Colorpoint in Seal, Blue, Chocolate, Cream, Lilac, and Red.

Ragdolls make good indoor pets, due to their placid nature. They don't need much exercise. Good news for wildlife-lovers is that Ragdolls do not seem to be interested in hunting. However, they are alert, intelligent, and respond well to training. They love family life and get on well with children. They will tolerate being picked up and carried around – just like a rag doll, in fact.

OPPOSITE: A Red point.

A Tabby Point.

SIBERIAN FOREST CAT

According to legend, the Siberian Forest Cats traditionally lived in Russian monasteries, where they patrolled the rafters on the lookout for intruders. Although fierce, the monks treated them as loving and loyal companions. It wasn't until the 1980s that a serious breeding program to standardize the type was begun. Although Siberians have been imported into the USA since 1990, so far TICA is the only major registry to recognize the breed.

This large, sturdily built cat has a broad head with a full, slightly rounded muzzle, and a well-rounded chin. The cat has large oval eyes and medium-sized ears with rounded tips. The inner ear has an abundance of ear tufts. The legs are thick and medium in length and the paws are large, round, and tufted. The tail is medium length and thick, with a rounded

tip. There is a tendency now for US bloodlines to be diverging somewhat in type from the traditional appearance, becoming more rounded rather than angled like that of a wildcat. Siberian Forest Cats are bred in a wide range of colors and varieties, with Tabbies, Tortoiseshells, and Bi-colors being relatively common. Smokes and Selfs are also seen.

The top coat is strong, plush and oily to ensure that the cat can survive in the harshest conditions. The undercoat is dense enough to give excellent protection against the elements, becoming thicker in cold weather.

The Siberian Forest Cat is an active and highly agile animal that is also sensible and resourceful. Although friendly, it also maintains an independent side to its nature.

SOMALI

The Somali is closely related to the Abyssinian, of which it is the semi-longhaired version. Semi-longhaired kittens have occasionally appeared in the litters of the shorthaired Abyssinian over several decades.

At first, these kittens were discarded and given away as pets, but it was eventually realized that a new breed was making a spontaneous appearance. The long fur was probably the result of a naturally long-established recessive gene within the breeding population. Somali to Somali pairings produce all Somali kittens, although their coats are shorter at this stage than those of adults.

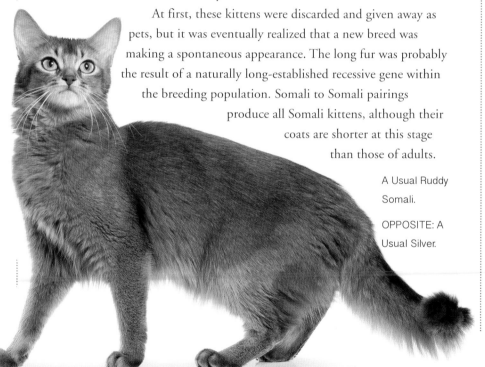

A Usual Ruddy Somali.

OPPOSITE: A Usual Silver.

Its firm, muscular body is of medium build with long legs and a long tail with a full brush of hair. The paws are oval and tufted. Ears are tufted, too, and are large, cupped, and wide-set. The head is a moderate wedge with a slight nose break in profile. The eyes are large, almond-shaped, and wide-set.

The coat is soft, fine, and dense and lies flat along the spine. The pattern of the Somali's coat is ticked with as many as 12 bands of color on each hair. It is easy to groom, though the ruff and tail need regular combing.

Colors include: Shaded Silver and Golden Silver. Non-Silver in Usual (Ruddy), Blue, Chocolate, Lilac, Sorrel, and Fawn. Silver in Usual Silver, Blue, Chocolate, Lilac, Sorrel, and fawn.

Not quite as outgoing as its Abyssinian relations, the Somali is nevertheless not

LEFT: A Blue.

OPPOSITE: A Usual Ruddy Kitten.

suited to confinement to the house, and being a natural hunter it thrives on activity. It is a charming and bright-eyed animal, with a cheeky demeanor, but is gentle and receptive to quiet handling and affection. It is soft-voiced and playful and makes a perfect companion pet.

A Fawn.

OPPOSITE: A Usual Ruddy.

TURKISH ANGORA

Angoras from Turkey first reached France in the 1500s. While the Turkish cat was an essential ingredient in the creation of today's Longhaired Persian, its type was not as popular. By the early 1900s, cross-breeding with other longhaired cats had led to the virtual extinction of the breed outside Turkey, and even in its homeland it was scarce. A breeding program was organized in Turkey by Ankara Zoo; then in the 1960s, the breed was imported into Sweden, the UK, and the USA from Turkey. It has now been renamed the Turkish Angora to avoid confusion with the modern re-creation bred from Oriental stock in the UK, but early references in the 1900s to the Angora refer to this cat.

An odd-eyed white.

OPPOSITE: A White kitten.

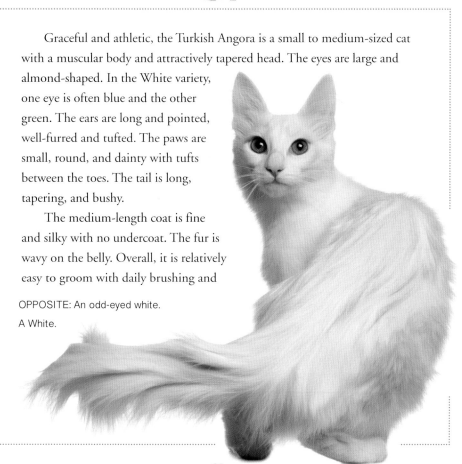

Graceful and athletic, the Turkish Angora is a small to medium-sized cat with a muscular body and attractively tapered head. The eyes are large and almond-shaped. In the White variety, one eye is often blue and the other green. The ears are long and pointed, well-furred and tufted. The paws are small, round, and dainty with tufts between the toes. The tail is long, tapering, and bushy.

The medium-length coat is fine and silky with no undercoat. The fur is wavy on the belly. Overall, it is relatively easy to groom with daily brushing and

OPPOSITE: An odd-eyed white.

A White.

combing. These cats molt heavily in the spring and subsequently, Turkish Angoras often resemble shorthaired cats through the warmer months of the year, but can still be distinguished by the longer fur on their tails.

Colors include: White, Black, Blue, Red, Cream, Tortoiseshell, Blue-cream, Bi-color, and Calico. Smoke in Black and Blue. Tabby in Silver and Brown.

The Turkish Angora is spirited with a sharp intelligence. It is often playful and enjoys games, but also likes peace and quiet. It is a companionable cat but can be aloof with strangers. It has a very loud voice and is an incessant talker. It can be destructive if left alone for any period of time.

A Brown Tabby.

OPPOSITE: An odd-eyed white.

TURKISH VAN

In 1955, two cats were brought to the UK from their native Lake Van area of eastern Turkey. The breed spread across Europe, but acceptance by registries took some time, eventually being achieved in 1969. Turkish Van cats were also introduced from Turkey directly to the USA, where they are now recognized by some associations.

A muscular cat with a long, sturdy body. The Turkish Van has a short, blunt, triangular head, a long, straight nose, and large, well-furred ears.

An Auburn.

OPPOSITE: A Black.

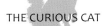

The eyes are large, rounded and highly expressive. The legs are medium in length with neat, tufted, well-rounded paws. The tail is a medium-length full brush in perfect proportion to the body.

The Turkish Van has a long, incredibly soft, silky coat with no woolly undercoat. The pattern is predominantly white, with colored markings on the face, and a white blaze. Colors are Auburn, Cream, Black, Tortie, and Tabby.

Renowned as the Swimming Cat, due to its habit of taking a dip in the waters of Lake Van, the Turkish Van will swim if given the opportunity, and unlike many cats, has no objection to being bathed. It is self-possessed, affectionate, and intelligent.

A Black Turkish Van.
OPPOSITE: A Cream Tabby.

"What greater gift than the love of a cat?"
Charles Dickens (1812-1870)

TO A CAT

Algernon Charles Swinburne (1837-1909)

Stately, kindly, lordly friend,
    Condescend
Here to sit by me, and turn
Glorious eyes that smile and burn,
Golden eyes, love's lustrous meed,
On the golden page I read.

All your wondrous wealth of hair,
    Dark and fair,
Silken-shaggy, soft and bright
As the clouds and beams of night
Pays my reverent hand's caress
Back with friendlier gentleness.

Dogs may fawn on all and some
    As they come;

You, a friend of loftier mind,
Answer friends alone in kind.
Just your foot upon my hand
Softly bids it understand.

LUCK CAT

Edith Södergran (1892-1923)

I have a luck cat in my arms,
it spins threads of luck.
Luck cat, luck cat,
make for me three things:
make for me a golden ring,
to tell me that I am lucky;
make for me a mirror
to tell me that I am beautiful;
make for me a fan
to waft away my
* cumbersome thoughts.*
Luck cat, luck cat,
spin for me some news of my
* future!*

SHORTHAIR GROUP

In the case of shorthairs, there is a noticeable difference between breeds originating from northern latitudes in Europe and those occurring nearer to the equator, which can be distinguished by having little undercoat. This is a reflection of the climate of their native environment, which is warmer and therefore means they need less insulation against the cold. As a result, their long outer guard hairs lie relatively smoothly, outlining the generally sleek profile of these athletic cats. It is also no coincidence that these breeds, evolved over the course of centuries, are smaller in size than those found in more northerly latitudes. It is easier for larger cats to maintain their core body temperature, thanks to their size, and this provides further evidence of how domestic cats have adapted relatively quickly to different environments.

An American Shorthair.

OPPOSITE: A Bengal.

ABYSSINIAN

This is one of the world's oldest cat breeds. First imported into the UK from Abyssinia (now Ethiopia) in Africa, as long ago as 1868, today's pedigree cats are not necessarily genetically linked to this individual. Its origins are, in fact, uncertain. Some claim that it was a Nile valley cat, worshipped by the ancient Egyptians. It certainly bears a close resemblance to the sacred cats carved and painted on Egyptian tombs. It also resembles the African wildcats, whose banded coats provide their owners with camouflage in the forest. Recognized as a breed in 1882, the Abyssinian was almost extinct in Britain at the start of the 20th century. Today, it is most popular in North America.

Medium size, slim, and muscular. The head is slightly rounded and wedge-shaped, gently curved in profile. The American

A Sorrel.

OPPOSITE: A playful Sorrel kitten.

Abyssinian has a shorter head and a more rounded profile than its European counterpart. The nose is medium-length, the ears large, and the almond-shaped eyes are also large and expressive. The tail is thick at the base and tapers.

The coat is soft, silky, fine-textured, and medium-length. All Abyssinians have unusual ticked coats, with two or three dark bands of color in them. The ticking is also known as agouti, referring to a particular rodent whose hair has similar color-banding down its length.

Colors include: Ruddy, Red or Sorrel, Blue, Fawn, Black Silver, and Blue Silver.

The earliest Abyssinians also showed tabby barring on their legs, but this has been removed over the generations by selective breeding, to the

OPPOSITE: A Ruddy.

A Fawn.

extent that the only evident tabby markings are now on the head, and the characteristic dark tip to the tail.

An active, intelligent cat that loves people; but it can be shy and mistrustful of strangers. It is, however, loyal and extremely affectionate towards its owners, though the Abyssinian tends to be more a climber than a lap-sitter. They are athletic and entertaining cats, fond of inventing games.

OPPOSITE: A Black Silver.

A Ruddy.

AMERICAN CURL

In 1981, a stray kitten appeared at a home in California, USA. The householder left food on the porch for it, which it ate, and adopted the house as its home. This female cat had a long, black, silky coat, and very unusual ears which curled back away from the face towards the back and center of the head. Later that year, the cat had a litter of kittens, two of which had the same curled ears. These cats were shown in

California in 1983 and the breed is now recognized in North America, the first American Curls reaching the UK in 1995. Outcrossing, which has produced a shorthaired Curl, ensures that genetic diversity continues to flourish within the breed. The curl itself has proved to be a dominant genetic trait, which means that kittens with ordinary ears born in a litter alongside American Curls will not carry the gene for this mutation, and are often described as Straight Ears. The curling causes these cats no apparent discomfort or problems.

The American Curl is a well-balanced, moderately muscled cat that is slender rather than massively built. The head is a modified wedge with a rounded muzzle and firm chin. The ears are moderately large, wide at the base, and open, curving back in a smooth arc when viewed from the front and rear. The ear tips are rounded. The eyes are walnut-shaped and slightly tilted. The paws are medium and rounded. The tail is equal to the length of the body, wide at the base, tapering, and plumed.

The coat is fine, silky, and flowing with minimal undercoat. These cats can be bred in a very wide range of colors and patterns.

The American Curl is an alert and active cat with a gentle, even disposition.

AMERICAN SHORTHAIR

The American Shorthair is very similar to British and European Shorthairs which are the oldest of the recognized shorthaired breeds. The breed's origins lie with the domestic cats taken to North America by settlers from Europe, dating back to the 1600s. At the beginning of the 20th century, some American breeders decided to develop this domestic cat's characteristics into a distinctive breed, as had happened in Europe with ordinary indigenous shorthairs. The first litter was from a mating of American and British Shorthairs. It was not until 1965 that the breed's name was changed from Domestic Shorthair to American Shorthair, in line with the names given to British and European Shorthairs.

A sturdy, medium to large cat with a strong, muscular body, and larger in size than an ordinary non-pedigree shorthair. The American Shorthair is not excessively cobby or rangy. The head is large with full cheeks and a square muzzle. The eyes are large, round, wide-set, and slightly slanted. The legs are firm-boned and the paws firm, full, and rounded with heavy pads. The tail is medium-length and heavy at the base, tapering to a blunt end.

The coat is short, dense, even, and firm in texture. It is somewhat heavier and thicker in winter. Grooming is easy, with regular combing all that is required to keep the coat in good condition.

Colors include: Solid in Black, White, Cream, Bi-color, Calico and Tortoiseshell. Tabby in Blue, Brown, Red, Cream, Cameo, Silver. Patched in Brown Patched, Blue Patched, and Silver Patched.

The American Shorthair is an easy-going, self-sufficient, no-nonsense cat. This even temperament ensures that the American Shorthair is an ideal family pet. It is bold, intelligent, inquisitive, and active and prefers to have access to outdoors. It has proved to be both healthy and hardy. It gets on well with other breeds and with dogs, displaying a very adaptable temperament. Its similarity to British and European Shorthairs has meant, however, that the popularity of this breed has not spread significantly outside North America.

AMERICAN WIREHAIR

The origins of the American Wirehair go back to a farm in Vermont, USA, in 1966. A red-and-white curly-coated male occurred as a spontaneous mutation in an American Shorthair litter. By 1969, a pure-breeding colony had been established and the breed was given official recognition by the CFA in 1977. The breed remains rare elsewhere in the world outside of the USA and Canada.

A medium to large cat with a rounded head, prominent cheekbones, and a well-developed muzzle. The eyes are large, round, bright, and clear. The American Wirehair comes in all colors and patterns except the colorpointed (Himalayan) series.

The unique, distinctive coat of the American Wirehair is springy, tight, and medium-length. The individual hairs are thinner than usual, and crimped, hooked or bent. Stroking the fur feels rather like touching an astrakhan hat. A cat with curly whiskers is highly prized. Minimal grooming is required, and an occasional soft brushing will keep the coat in top condition. The gentle use of a rubber brush will help to remove dead hair during a molt.

The American Wirehair is very positive and inquisitive, sometimes to the point of bossiness – indeed, it is said to rule the home and cats of other breeds with an 'iron paw.' However, it is also said to be a breed that never seems to stop purring! In addition, it is rarely destructive and enjoys being handled.

BENGAL

The Bengal is the result of the crossing of the Asian Leopard Cat with domestic cats in order to produce a wild-looking cat with a docile temperament. A rigid breeding program was established in the 1980s to establish that the cat's wild tendencies had been bred out and that it was now suitable as a domestic pet. Early crosses were to non-pedigrees, but when the spotted leopard-like coat appeared, Bengals were crossed with Egyptian Maus and Ocicats. This practice is no longer condoned by most breeders.

Resembling a spotted Asian Leopard Cat, the Bengal is large, robust, and muscular. The head is a medium wedge shape and rather small in proportion to the body. The profile has a gentle curve from the forehead to the bridge of the nose and a prominent brow. The nose is large and broad, and the eyes are large and almond-shaped. It has short ears.

Unlike any other domestic cat, the Bengal's thick, luxuriant coat glitters as if sprinkled with gold dust. The silky texture is more like that of a wildcat's pelt than a domestic cat's fur.

Bengals have been bred with both spotted and so-called marbled tabby markings, as well as Selfs.

Colors include: Brown Tabby, Blue-eyed Snow, Brown Snow, and Blue.

A friendly, loving, alert, curious and intelligent cat, the Bengal has little fear of other cats, or any other animal. Bengals are not afraid of water. Indeed, they like to play with it, and also with toys. They are great climbers and love heights.

"Intelligence in the cat is underrated."

Louis Wain (1880-1939)

THE TIGER

William Blake (1757-1827)

Tiger Tiger, burning bright,
In the forests of the night;
What immortal hand or eye,
Could frame thy fearful symmetry?

In what distant deeps or skies.
Burnt the fire of thine eyes?
On what wings dare he aspire?
What the hand, dare seize the fire?

And what shoulder, & what art,
Could twist the sinews of thy heart?
And when thy heart began to beat,
What dread hand? & what dread feet?

What the hammer? what the chain,
In what furnace was thy brain?
What the anvil? what dread grasp,
Dare its deadly terrors clasp!

When the stars threw down their spears
And water'd heaven with their tears:
Did he smile his work to see?
Did he who made the Lamb make thee?

Tiger Tiger burning bright,
In the forests of the night:
What immortal hand or eye,
Dare frame thy fearful symmetry?

BOMBAY

The Bombay is named in honor of the Indian city of that name because of the resemblance the cat bears to the black panther – a native of India. In the 1950s, an American breeder tried to recreate the look of the panther by crossing black American Shorthairs and Sable Burmese. The Bombay was first recognized in the mid 1970s. In the UK, black British Shorthairs were mated with Burmese and became part of the Asian Group breeding program.

The cat has a medium-sized, muscular body with a rounded head and full face. It has a short snub nose and a firm chin. The medium-sized ears have slightly rounded tips and are tilted slightly forwards, giving the cat an alert expression. The eyes are large, round, and copper-colored. The legs are in proportion to the body and the paws are round. Everything about the cat is black, from the nose to the paw pads.

The short, shiny coat is very close-lying, with a sheen like jet black patent leather, hence the cat's nickname in America: 'the patent-leather kid with new-penny eyes.' The fur must be jet black to the tips. The coat needs very little grooming to keep it in top condition; buffing with a silk scarf or velvet grooming mitt will enhance the coat's glossy sheen.

The Bombay has a typically Burmese temperament, being good-tempered – even sedate. But it is gregarious, affectionate, and requires lots of attention. It makes a very good pet.

BRITISH SHORTHAIR

This breed probably stems from the first domestic cats that arrived in Britain with the Romans in the Ist century AD. The modern breed was developed in the 1880s from farm, street, and domestic cats in the UK, in response to the growing interest in showing cats which began at this stage. The breed was in decline by the turn of the 20th century, however, due to the rise in popularity of more exotic breeds for show purposes, notably Persian Longhairs, and had almost died out by the 1950s. At that time, matings with Blue Persians then resulted in the British Shorthairs being developed in

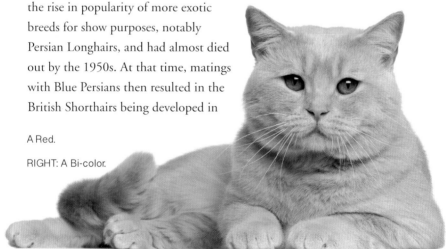

A Red.

RIGHT: A Bi-color.

terms of their size and appearance, and helped them to regain their popularity. Similar breeding programs over recent years have led to the introduction of new color variants to the breed, such as Chocolate and Lilac, as well as the creation of a Colorpoint lineage, which combines the markings of the Colorpoint Longhair (Himalayan) breed with the appearance of the British Shorthair. Nowadays, the British Shorthair has become the third largest group of registered pedigree cats in the UK, thanks partly to the exposure which the breed has received as a result of its use in various advertising campaigns for cat food.

The Shorthair's compact, well balanced, and powerful body is surprisingly heavy. The chest is full and broad. Legs are short and strong with large, rounded paws. The tail is thick at the base and rounded at the tip. The head is very broad and round with well developed cheeks. The eyes are large and round, while the ears are small.

The coat is short, thick, and fine. Numerous guard hairs give the coat a distinctive, crisp feel. The protective undercoat insulates the cat from the cold. Daily grooming with a comb will keep the coat in prime condition, although, unlike the Longhair, this is not essential.

Colors include: Solid in Black, White, Orange-eyed White, Cream, and Blue. Tortoiseshell in Blue-cream, Chocolate, Lilac, Tortie-and-white, and Blue Tortie-and-white. Tabby in Classic, Mackerel, and Spotted with colors in Brown, Red, Silver, Blue, and Cream. Tipped in Black (silver) and Golden (non-silver). Other colors include Black Smoke, Blue Smoke, Colorpointed, and Bi-color.

OPPOSITE: A Chocolate.
A Blue.

Its intelligent yet phlegmatic nature makes the British Shorthair a solid and dependable feline companion, responding readily to affection. It is also self-possessed and self-reliant, undemanding and friendly. The breed may appear to be a cuddly cross between a cat and a teddy bear, but they are also skilled hunters, and toms can be determined fighters due to their strong territorial instincts. Neutering will modify these aggressive tendencies towards other cats, but should not be carried out too early, before the distinctive fleshy pads, called jowls, have developed around the face. This creates what has been likened to a double-chinned appearance, which would otherwise not appear, as they only develop in mature toms.

OPPOSITE: A Lilac.
A Golden Tipped.

BURMESE

In the early 1930s, a Siamese hybrid female, named Wong Mau, was taken from Rangoon in Burma (now Myanmar) to the USA and mated with a Seal Point Siamese. Some of the resulting offspring were dark brown and formed the beginnings of the official pedigree Burmese. The breed was registered in 1936, and then in 1952 it was recognized in the UK. Since then, the breed has developed to slightly different standards on opposite sides of the Atlantic, with the result that there are now different classes at many cat shows in North America, catering separately for Burmese and also Burmese of European appearance.

Despite having a genetic pattern almost identical to the Siamese, the Burmese is much more compactly built, not having been subsequently evolved on such extreme lines.

In fact, these cats approximate more closely in type to early Siamese, compared with their contemporary cousins. The nose has an obvious break in its line. The head is round with very full cheeks. The eyes are large, round and yellow to gold in color. The cats have well-proportioned legs and neat, oval paws. The tail is straight and of medium length, tapering to a rounded tip. Those of US origins are more cobby in shape, a fact emphasized by their legs, which are slightly shorter than those of their European counterparts, which have a more angular profile overall, and oval-shaped eyes.

The short, fine, glossy coat is close-lying and needs very little grooming to keep it in top condition.

Colors include: Solid in Red, Cream, Sable, Blue, and Chocolate. Tortoiseshell (Tortie) in Seal, Blue-cream, Chocolate, and Lilac-cream.

The Burmese has a sunny disposition and keen intelligence. It is active, inquisitive, and adaptable. However, it does not like being left alone and can be strong-willed. It is less vocal and demonstrative than other Oriental breeds. These cats remain playful all their adult lives and need a devoted human family surrounding them.

BURMILLA

An accidental mating between a lilac Burmese female and a Chinchilla Silver male in 1981 resulted in the birth of attractive shaded-silver female kittens. They were all of shorthaired Burmese type with the stunning

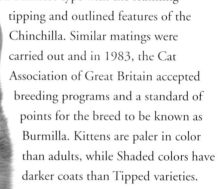

tipping and outlined features of the Chinchilla. Similar matings were carried out and in 1983, the Cat Association of Great Britain accepted breeding programs and a standard of points for the breed to be known as Burmilla. Kittens are paler in color than adults, while Shaded colors have darker coats than Tipped varieties.

The female Burmilla is markedly smaller and daintier than the male, but the body type is generally medium-sized and straight-backed. Legs are long and sturdy with neat, oval paws. The Burmilla carries its tail high and proud. The head is a medium wedge, gently rounded at the top and the ears are large. The large, expressive eyes are outlined with dark 'eyeliner.' The lips and nose leather are similarly outlined. The tail is medium to long, fairly thick at the base, and tapering slightly to a rounded tip.

The coat is short, dense, soft, and glossy, slightly longer than the Burmese and with enough undercoat to give it a slight lift. The Burmilla's most impressive feature is the sparkling shading or tipping on the coat. It is best to groom the dense coat with a rubber brush to loosen dead hairs before combing.

Color varieties include: Shaded or Tipped in Black, Blue, Brown, Chocolate, Lilac, Red, Cream, Red Tortie, Blue Tortie, Brown Tortie, Chocolate Tortie, and Lilac Tortie.

The Burmilla is stable and dignified, but inquisitive and sociable, too, though less boisterous than the typical Burmese. However, they are more sociable than Longhairs. They are playful and very affectionate.

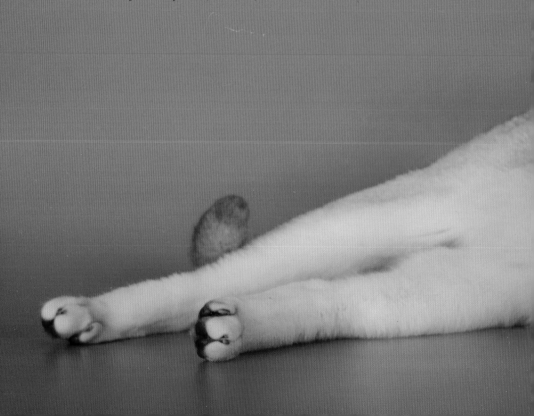

"I like cats.... When I meet a cat, I say, "Poor Pussy!" and stoop down and tickle the side of its head; and the cat sticks up its tail in a rigid, cast-iron manner, arches its back, and wipes its nose up against my trousers; and all is gentleness and peace."

Jerome K. Jerome (1859-1927)

CHARTREUX

Native to France, this breed is said to have been bred as long ago as the 16th century near the French town of Grenoble, at the Monastery of La Grande Chartreuse (which was also responsible for the liqueur of that name). In the 1930s, a French vet suggested that the breed should have its own scientific name. The Chartreux reached North America in the 1970s, but is not bred in many European countries. This breed should not be confused with the British Blue or the European Shorthaired Blue.

Well-proportioned but stocky, with short legs and large, muscular shoulders, the Chartreux is rather lighter than its British counterpart, the British Blue Shorthair. Its head is large and round with well-developed cheeks and a short, strong neck. Eyes are

large and open, not too rounded, and with the outer corners slightly uptilted. Eye color is vivid deep yellow to vivid deep copper. Ears are medium-sized and set high on the head. The paws are large and the tail is medium-length with a rounded tip.

The coat is dense, soft, and plush with a slightly woolly undercoat and a glossy appearance. Daily grooming with a comb is needed to keep the undercoat in good condition, while brushing enhances the way in which the coat characteristically stands away from the body.

A calm, affectionate, intelligent, and attentive cat. It is less talkative than most breeds, with a high-pitched miaow and an infrequently used chirp. The cat will happily live confined to the house, so it is a suitable pet for an apartment-dweller.

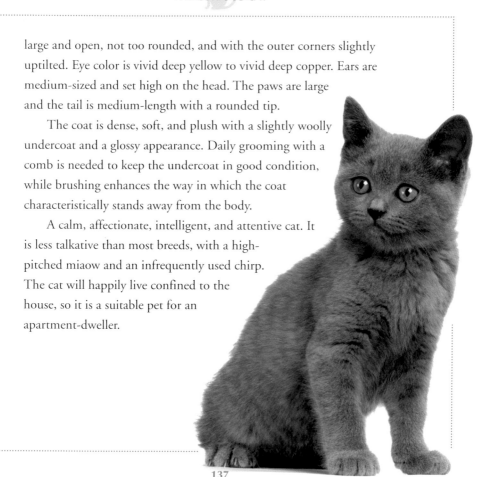

CORNISH REX

The first recorded Cornish Rex kitten was born in 1950 in Cornwall, England. The kitten, named Kallibunker, was red with a white chest and belly and its fur was closely waved. It was mated with its mother, and the resulting litter contained two curly-coated kittens. Descendants were then backcrossed to Rex cats to create the recessive curly coat. The breed was officially recognized in 1967 in the UK and 1979 in the USA.

The Cornish Rex is medium-sized, hard-bodied, muscular, and slender, with a curving back and huge ears set high on a disproportionately small head. The arched back is set on fine, lean legs. The American standard for these cats requires a 'tucked-up' torso that gives the cat the appearance of a whippet.

The most unusual feature of the Cornish Rex is its short, plush, regularly-waved coat. Because it lacks guard hairs, the coat is soft and velvety to touch. The whiskers and eyebrows are crinkled. The curly coat does not shed hair, making it easy to groom by stroking.

Affectionate and people-oriented, the Cornish Rex wags its tail to show that it is happy. These cats are very lively, playful, and agile, capable of leaping effortlessly from ground to shoulder height. They enjoy games of fetch, catch, and batting objects with their paws.

To widen the gene pool and ensure stamina in the Cornish Rex as a breed, the first breeders outcrossed to other breeds that had the desired conformation. Foreign breeds, such as the Havana, Russian Blue, Burmese, and

Siamese were selected, especially in North America, whereas British Shorthairs were used for this purpose in the UK. All the offspring of Cornish Rex and non-rexed cats resulted in cats with normal coats. All carried the recessive gene for the curly coat and when these cats matured and were mated, approximately half the litter on average would be comprised of curly-coated kittens. The various colors and coat patterns of the cats selected for the original outcrosses resulted in a wide range of color varieties in the Cornish Rex breed, and breeders soon began to show their preferences for certain colors and combinations of colors.

DEVON REX

In 1960, in Devon, England, a curly-coated feral male was mated with a stray, straight-haired female. The litter included one curly-coated male, named Kirlee, showing that the curly hair gene was recessive. The parents were almost certainly related, and inbreeding was needed to perpetuate the Devon Rex. By 1970, the breed had been recognized in the UK. It was not until 1979 that it was recognized in the USA.

The Devon Rex shares the muscular build, slim legs, and long, whip-like tail of the Cornish Rex, but it is broad-chested, and has a flat forehead, prominent cheekbones, and a crinkled brow. Its coat runs in a rippled pattern rather than wavy like the Cornish Rex, which is a quite separate mutation, in spite of both breeds arising in neighboring counties in the south-west of England. The face of the Devon Rex is

wide with large, round eyes, prominent, brittle whiskers, and huge, low-set ears. These cats are commonly nicknamed 'poodle cats' because of their wavy coats and habit of wagging their tails. The Devon has a

quizzical impish expression, which some people regard as almost extraterrestrial.

The Devon Rex coat is generally less dense and more coarse and curly than that of the Cornish Rex and, without careful breeding, very sparse coats can result. Kittens in particular often have relatively sparse coats. Even the whiskers are affected and, being crinkled, tend to break more easily than normal. The coat requires gentle stroking with a soft mitt rather than a brush. A piece of silk is often favored by exhibitors of Devon Rexes to give a good gloss to the coat. All coat colors, patterns, and color combinations are allowed in the case of this breed.

This is certainly a cat for the connoisseur. Even more playful than the Cornish Rex, the Devon Rex loves fooling around. It can be extremely mischievous and demanding of human attention, but is extremely loving and intelligent.

EGYPTIAN MAU

Not only can images of a spotted tabby cat be seen in the wall paintings and scrolls of ancient Egypt, but its descendents may still be seen on the streets of Cairo today. Many believe that the Egyptian Maus are direct descendents of the African wildcats that they more closely resemble than any other domestic cat. Maus were probably introduced into Europe aboard the ships of Phoenician traders more than 2,000 years ago. The current stock in the USA is descended from three Maus imported into the USA in the 1950s by an exiled Russian princess.

The Egyptian Mau is medium-sized, long, and graceful, with a head that is a slightly rounded wedge-shape. The medium to large ears are alert and slightly

Silver Egyptian Maus.

146

pointed and the inner ear is a delicate shell pink. Legs are in proportion to the body and the paws are small and slightly oval. The tail is thick at the base and slightly tapered.

The coat is short and silky with random spots that vary in size and shape. The spots form a contrast to the lighter background coat that comes in just three colors: Silver, Bronze and Black Smoke. The hair has two or more bands of ticking, separated by lighter bands. The coat is easy to maintain but needs regular grooming.

These cats are alert, affectionate and intelligent, but rather shy. The Egyptian Mau is good with children but dislikes strangers. It is happiest given plenty of space for jumping, climbing, and hunting.

OPPOSITE: A Bronze.

A Black Smoke.

EUROPEAN SHORTHAIR

The first European Shorthairs were descended from cats introduced to Northern Europe nearly 2,000 years ago by Roman soldiers, who brought them to kill rats in their food stores. Until 1982, European Shorthairs were classified with British Shorthairs. FIFe then gave the breed its own category and it began effectively as a ready-made breed, with a full range of colors, established type, and breeding stock, with known histories. The breed is now being selectively bred, this trend having started in Scandinavia, and no British Shorthair crosses are now being permitted in the pedigree of these cats, nor are Persian Longhairs, used in the past to increase the size of the breed. It is not recognized by the GCCF or major breed registries outside Europe.

More elegant than the British Shorthair, emphasis in the European Shorthair lies in its lithe muscularity rather than round cobbiness. Its face is slightly longer and less heavily jowled than its British cousin's. The body is strong and broad-chested, with fairly long, well-boned legs, and firm, rounded paws. The tail is in proportion to the body and rounded at the tip. Largish ears are upright with rounded tips and set fairly wide apart. The eyes are large, round, and well spaced.

The all-weather coat is short and dense, with a crisp texture. It stands away from the body. Grooming is easy. Regular brushing to keep the undercoat in good condition is all that is necessary.

Colors include: Solid in White, Black, Blue, Red, and Cream. Tortoiseshell (Tortie) in Smoke, Black and Blue. Tabby in Black, Blue, Red,

Cream, Black Tortie, Blue Tortie, Silver, and Mackerel. Non-Tabby in Bi-color, Van-patterned, Tabby Van, Tortie Van, Harlequin, and Tabby Bi-color.

The European Shorthair is particularly adaptable, independent, and bright, and therefore must not be confined indoors. It is also placid and affectionate and relatively quiet, thus making it an ideal family pet.

"A countryman between two lawyers is like a fish between two cats."

Benjamin Franklin (1706-1790)

EXOTIC SHORTHAIR

The breed was developed in the mid 1960s, with the aim of producing a shorthaired Persian cat. Thus Persians were crossed with various shorthairs and the product was a shorthaired cat that required minimal grooming and had the Persian's gentle nature. It has all the physical characteristics of the Persian cat, and is available in the same colors and variations. Some Exotic Shorthairs have also inherited the defects of the Persians, so in North America, only outcrosses with American Shorthairs and Persians are allowed. Elsewhere, other breeds may sometimes be used.

The Exotic Shorthair is of medium to large build and cobby. The head is round and massive and set on a short, thick neck. The cat has full cheeks and broad,

A Tortie Bi-color.
OPPOSITE: A Tabby Bi-color.

powerful jaws. The eyes are large, round, and bright. The nose is short and stubby, and the ears are small and blunt, set wide apart and leaning slightly forward.

The coat is not quite short but not semi-long either. It is slightly longer than other shorthairs' but not long enough to flow. The texture is dense, plush, soft, and lively. It is not flat or close-lying. Grooming is easy, though thorough brushing and combing a couple of times a week is necessary. Shining fur is achieved by correct feeding. The coat occurs in all colors found in American Shorthairs and Persians.

All solid colors are permitted, as well as Tabby, Tortoiseshell, Bi-color, Colorpoint, Smoke, and Chinchilla.

The Exotic Shorthair has the placidity and dignity of the Persian, yet also has a playful and affectionate side to its nature. It is patient with children and is content to be an indoor cat. It has the soft, squeaky voice of its parent breed.

OPPOSITE: A Black Smoke.

A Tortoiseshell kitten.

HAVANA BROWN

For a hundred years, breeders had been trying to develop an all-brown cat. In the 1950s, British cat breeders developed a solid chocolate of Siamese type from the accidental mating of a black non-pedigree cat and a Chocolate Point Siamese. The color was called Havana, but the breed was registered in the UK as the Chestnut Brown Foreign Shorthair, being known under this name until the 1970s. Havana Browns were also exported to the US. They were registered as Havana Browns until 1973, when the CFA accepted the Oriental Shorthair breed. From then on these imports were registered as Chestnut Oriental Shorthairs. The

unusual description of Havana was chosen because of the striking similarity between the color of these cats and that of the rabbit breed which was already known by this name.

The head is shaped like the Siamese's, being longer than it is wide. The ears are large and round and slightly pricked to give an alert appearance. The oval eyes are a vivid green. The body is medium-sized, firm, and muscular, and the medium-length tail tapers gently to a slightly pointed tip. The males are usually larger than the females. All Havana Browns are a warm chestnut brown color. There is now a distinct difference in appearance between these cats in North America and Europe, with those of North American origins having a less extreme appearance, with a more rounded head-shape than their European counterparts. This is because Siamese have not played such a significant role in their development.

The coat is short to medium in length, smooth and lustrous, and is easy to maintain with the minimum of grooming. Combing will remove any loose hairs.

A highly playful, athletic, and energetic cat, fond of games and an excellent climber, the Havana Brown is a sweet-natured and sociable cat. It thrives on plenty of affection and attention. These cats are highly intelligent and like investigating new things, pawing, and playing with objects. It is less vocal than a Siamese and makes an excellent pet.

JAPANESE BOBTAIL

This is a breed that has existed in Japan for many centuries. The Japanese Bobtail is considered to be a symbol of domestic good fortune and probably originated from domesticated shorthaired cats that had mutated into a tailless version. It was not until after World War II that the Bobtail was discovered by the international cat fancying world. In 1963, American judges visiting a show in Japan, spotted a Bobtail, and were impressed. Five years later, an American breeder took 38 Bobtails back to the USA from Japan and the breed became accepted for show purposes in 1978 by the CFA. The breed is also now recognized in the UK, but is virtually unknown there at present.

The Japanese Bobtail's distinctive tail is just 3–4-inches (8–10-cm) long. It is normally curled up in a bob, but can be held upright when the cat is alert or advertising its presence. The body is medium-sized, slim but well-muscled. The head is pointed, with high cheekbones, and slanted eyes that produce a unique profile. The Bobtail is available in most colors and patterns. In Japan, the Van-patterned Tortie-and-White, known as *Mi-ke* (meaning three colors) is the most prized. There is also a long-coated version of this breed, which was recognized separately from its short-coated counterpart

in the USA during 1991. These particular cats appear to be naturally more common in northern parts of Japan, with their tails resembling fluffy pompoms.

The coat is medium in length, soft, and silky with no undercoat and little shedding of hair. Grooming is easy with regular combing.

Friendly, curious, and playful, and being very people-oriented, Bobtails make ideal family pets. They often have an endearing habit of raising one paw as if in greeting. They have a soft voice with a range of sounds. Bobtails enjoy swimming and can also be taught to retrieve.

"Thousands of years ago, cats were worshipped as gods. Cats have never forgotten this."

Anonymous

KORAT

Alongside the Siamese, the Korat is one of the distinctive cats of Thailand, and is considered a good-luck charm in its native land. A pair of Korats is a traditional wedding present, intended to bestow long life, wealth and happiness. Known since at least the 14th century, it is described in the *Cat Book of Poems*, a 16th-century manuscript of the ancient Thai kingdom of Ayutthaya. In the 20th century, Korats captured the attention of US servicemen in Thailand, and the first examples of the breed were imported into the USA in 1959. It gained official recognition in 1966, but was not introduced into Europe until 1972.

A strikingly handsome cat with large and piercing green eyes which are round and prominent when open, but appear slanted when closed. The Korat's head is large and heart-shaped, giving it a soft appearance. The chin is firm and rounded. The ears are large with rounded tips, set high on the head, giving the cat an alert expression. The Korat's body is well-muscled and strong. Blue of a silvery shade is the traditionally accepted color form in the West, although recently, odd lilac Korats have been bred in Europe, cropping up unexpectedly in litters of ordinary Korats. In the UK, these cats are officially described as the Thai Lilacs of Korat Type, following a ruling by the GCCF in 1998, although they are not yet recognized for show purposes.

The glossy, fine, close-lying coat is short, with no undercoat. The coat is blue, with the guard hairs tipped in silver, giving it an intense sheen. Grooming is minimal. A cloth or comb run over the coat is all that is needed to keep it smooth.

These cats have a strong personality and can be demanding. They like to have their own way and need plenty of attention. They are extremely playful and respond well to training.

LAPERM

In 1986, on a farm in Oregon, USA, a litter of six kittens was born to a farm cat. One of the kittens was born bald. Within eight weeks, the kitten began to grow very soft, curly hair. By four months, it had a full coat of curly hair. It was later mated and gave birth to five male kittens, all bald at birth, like their mother had been. As the breeding program progressed, it became clear that the curly gene was dominant and could be carried by both males and females. The owner gave the cats the breed name 'LaPerm,' signifying wavy or rippled. Of the major registries, only TICA and the CFA have recognized the breed, this status first being accorded to the breed in 1995.

Interestingly, today's LaPerm kittens are not normally bald at birth, which could have served to lessen their chances of survival by leaving them more vulnerable to becoming chilled. Nevertheless, the breed still remains essentially unknown outside North America.

The face and head is somewhat triangular in shape with wide-set ears, relatively large whisker pads, and large, expressive eyes. LaPerms can also boast a splendid set of curly whiskers and eyebrows.

The coat can form waves or ringlets that range from tight to long corkscrew curls, depending on whether the cat is short- or long-coated. The coat generally stands away from the body, parting down the middle. Grooming is minimal because the coat does not easily mat. Because of the appearance of its coat, the breed is still sometimes known as the Alpaca Cat, the alpaca being a relative of the shaggy-coated llama, highly prized for the quality of its wool.

LaPerms are gentle and affectionate but also very active. However, unlike many energetic breeds, these cats are also content to be lap cats. They seek human contact and will purr as soon as they see you, making them probably the most sociable breed of all. Generally they are quiet, but they can be vocal when seeking attention.

MANX

This unusual cat with no tail hails from the Isle of Man, UK. The lack of a tail, however, is a genetic mutation that occurs occasionally in all animals. In isolated populations, such as on islands, there is a greater chance that such a gene will be perpetuated. The original mutation must have occurred many years ago, for Manx cats have been known for a long time to a specialist breed club first established in Britain in 1901. Although it is an old breed, Manx cats remain rare. Breeders have to cross tailless Manx with Manx that have tails as there is a lethal genetic factor involved in Rumpy-to-Rumpy pairings, which will cause some of the kittens to die at or shortly after birth.

The breed's most obvious characteristic is its frequent lack of a tail and rounded body shape. The only acceptable form for showing is the Rumpy, in which there is a slight hollow on the rump where the tail should be. There are also three recognized varieties with residual tails of varying lengths. The Rumpy Riser has only a vestigial knob for a tail, the Stumpy has a short tail, while the Longy has a shortened but otherwise normal tail. Manx cats also have a distinctive 'bunny-hop' gait, caused by the lack of a tail combined with hind legs that are longer than the front legs.

The Manx's coat is short, dense, and double, giving a padded quality due to the comparatively long, open outer coat, and the close, cottony undercoat. Regular grooming is essential.

Colors include: Solid in Black, Blue, Red, and Cream. Tortoiseshell in Blue-cream, Calico, and Dilute Calico. Chinchilla in Shaded Silver, Black Smoke, and Blue Smoke. Tabby in Classic and Mackerel in Brown, Blue, Red, Cream, Cameo, and Silver.

These cats are affectionate, calm, quiet and intelligent. They are not particularly active and prefer sitting with their owner to being out of doors.

A Rumpy Riser Brown
Tabby kitten.

MUNCHKIN

The Munchkin originated as a spontaneous genetic mutation in Louisiana, USA, in 1983. This resulted in a cat with disproportionately short legs that have caused it to be the subject of considerable controversy. The Munchkin cat was recognized as a new breed by TICA in 1995. Although the Munchkin is new to breed associations, cats with short legs were known in Europe during the first part of the 20th century, but seem to have died out. Now, demand for Munchkins far exceeds the

supply, and they are gradually becoming more numerous in Europe as well as North America.

The body and head are medium-sized, the ears quite large and triangular, and the eyes large and walnut-shaped. The legs are significantly shorter than those of other cats, but straight with slightly turned-out paws. The tail is of medium thickness, tapering to a rounded tip.

Both longhaired and shorthaired varieties are available.

The Munchkin is available in a variety of colors and patterns. Tabbies and bi-colors are more common than oriental shades and patterns.

Despite the short legs, Munchkins can run extremely fast. They are able to climb trees as well as any other cat; however, they do not jump as high because the shorter back legs do not give the same degree of leverage. Munchkins are playful, outgoing and love to be handled. They are very sociable and intelligent, and enjoy company. Friendly and self-assured, the Munchkin gets on well with other pets, too.

OCICAT

The first kitten of this breed appeared in the 1960s as the result of the accidental mating of a hybrid Abyssinian-Siamese female with a Chocolate Point Siamese male. The spotted pattern of the kitten reminded its breeder's daughter of a baby ocelot, and she decided to produce similar cats which were eventually recognized as a separate breed called the Ocicat. It obtained full championship status in North America in 1987. A similar breeding program has seen the Ocicat being created on similar lines in Europe, where it is currently growing in popularity.

The Ocicat is a rather large, but well-proportioned cat, powerful and agile with a typical 'wildcat' appearance. The head is wedge-shaped with clear, definite markings including the characteristic tabby M on the forehead. It has a broad muzzle and strong chin. The ears are large and alert. The Ocicat is remarkable for its striking, almond-shaped eyes. The long body is athletic and muscular, the legs are long and the tail fairly long and slightly tapered. Originally, the number of Ocicat colors was restricted, but more colors were introduced by crossing examples of the breed with American Shorthairs. The range of colors now includes Chocolate, Blue, Lavender, and Fawn, as well as Silver and Smoke variants.

The Ocicat's coat is short and smooth, satiny and lustrous. All hairs, except those on the tip of the tail, are banded. Hairs in the ground color are tipped with a lighter color. The pattern is that of a spotted tabby cat, although the spotted patterning becomes less obvious during a molt. The tail should always end in a dark tip, reflecting the true coat color of the individual. Gentle brushing is all that is required by way of grooming.

Ocicats are loving and gentle, inquisitive and playful, and make excellent pets. They are outgoing and are friendly towards strangers and even dogs. They love to explore their surroundings and need plenty of opportunity for climbing.

NEBELUNG

The Nebelung – whose name means 'mist-creature' in German – is a new, longhaired version of the Russian Blue that was developed in the USA in the 1980s. In 1987, the breed was accepted by TICA and it was also recognized by the TCA in 1990; since then other major registries have accepted it also. Although the Nebelung is gaining popularity, it is still not very well known.

Similar in all respects to the Russian Blue except for the coat length, the Nebelung is a rather delicate-looking cat, with a long body, legs, and tail, and green eyes.

The double coat is long, fine, and soft. The guard hairs are silver-tipped. Daily grooming is required.

The Nebelung is calm, gentle, and can be playful. Although the Nebelung is loving and affectionate, it may not be the best choice for a family with small children, because it is timid and has a reserved personality.

Blue is most the common color, although there is also a White variety.

"I believe cats to be spirits come to earth. A cat, I am sure, could walk on a cloud without coming through."

Jules Verne (1828-1905)

ORIENTAL

Oriental cats first became popular in the early 1960s when a small number of breeders began mating Siamese with indigenous cats, such as the British, European and American Shorthairs, to produce a wide range of colors and patterns. They have since only been outcrossed to Siamese. The care taken with the selection of their foundation stock ensures strength, stamina, and good temperament, as well as beauty. This is one of the most diverse of all cat breeds and groups.

By and large, Oriental cats are identical to Siamese cats in all respects except for having all-over coat color and pattern rather than the Siamese colorpoints on face, ears, tail and legs. Unlike the Siamese, most Orientals do not have blue eyes. Their appearance is almost canine – moving as they do like a whippet, and with a whip-like tail.

The Oriental cat's coat has a short, fine texture that is glossy and close-lying. They are naturally very clean cats and minimal grooming is required. Buffing with a soft glove or silk scarf is recommended.

Colors include: Solid in Oriental White, Foreign White, Siamese White, Black, Blue, Chocolate, Lilac, Cinnamon, Caramel, Fawn, Red, and Cream. Tortoiseshell in Black, Blue, Chocolate, Lilac, Cinnamon, and Caramel. Tabby in Black, Blue, Chocolate, Lilac, Cream, Cinnamon, Caramel, Fawn, Silver, and Tortie. There are also Smoke, Shaded, Tipped and Bi-color varieties.

This is an extrovert cat, intelligent, inquisitive, and very affectionate. It is active and playful and hates being left alone for long periods. The Oriental is as talkative as a Siamese, but its voice is a little quieter. Many people find that the cat's response to humans is much like that of a dog. Orientals will often run to greet their owners on their return home, and demand to be played with.

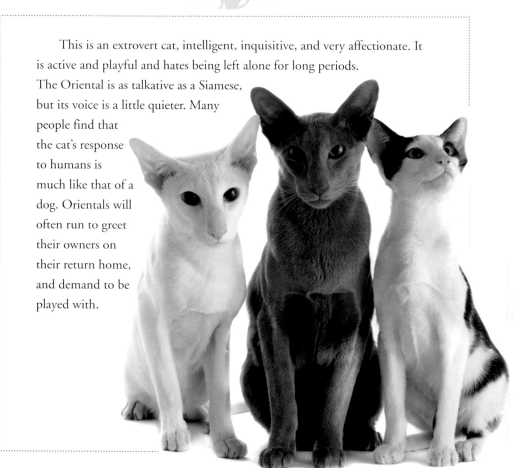

RAGAMUFFIN

Ragamuffins are closely associated with their ancestors, the Ragdolls. They were bred specifically for their sweet temperament and were designated as a separate breed in 1994. Ragdolls are recognized for competition only in limited colors, but the Ragamuffin is available in many colors, including all pointed color varieties.

The head is a medium-sized, broad, modified wedge. The nose is medium and the eyes are large, oval, expressive, and inquisitive. Ears are medium-sized, with a slight forward tilt, and rounded tips. The very large body is heavy, firm, and muscular with a full chest. The tail is long and fluffy with a slight taper and carried higher than the back.

The coat is luxuriantly long or semi-long, plush and silky, and shorter on the face. The coat length varies slightly, but in general it is low-maintenance compared to that of other longhaired breeds.

Colors include: All pointed varieties in Red, Tortie, Mink, Sepia, Seal, Blue, Chocolate, and Lilac. All colors of Persians in Solid, Mitted, and Parti-color. Selfs, Tabbies, Torties, and Blue-eyed pointed varieties are also available.

Ragamuffins make ideal pets for the first-time cat owner. They are one of the most relaxed, perfectly happy cats you are ever likely to encounter, with an unusually docile and warm disposition. They are true people-loving cats and get along well with children and other pets, and they love to be where the action is. They also tend to be soft-pawed (they rarely put out their claws). The Ragamuffin is suitable only as an indoor pet. They don't possess the defense instincts of most other cats, so they need protection.

RUSSIAN BLUE

Legend has it that the Russian Blue is a descendant of ships' cats brought from the White Sea in northern Russia to Britain in the 1800s. The modern Russian Blue contains bloodlines derived in part from British Blues and from Blue Point Siamese, consequences of Swedish and British efforts to revive the breed in the 1950s following its near extinction during World War II. Blue was the original coat color and is preferred by traditionalists, but black and white coats are also available, especially in Europe and New Zealand.

The Russian Blue is medium in size with a body that is well-muscled but finer-boned than other shorthairs. The legs are long and the tail is of medium length and thickness. The head is wedge-shaped with a nose of medium length and a level chin. The ears are large and

pointed with very little hair inside or out. The eyes are large, almond-shaped, widely spaced, and vivid green in color.

The soft, dense, insulating double coat is thick and lustrous, its density causing the coat to stand out from the body. Minimal grooming is required. Some breeders say the coat looks best if it is never brushed.

A cautious cat, the Russian Blue dislikes changes in its environment and is shy with strangers. It needs the company of humans or other pets. A gentle breed, the Russian Blue is among the least destructive of all cats, and considered by many cat fanciers to be an ideal indoor companion. It is the perfect companion for flat-dwellers.

SAVANNAH

The Savannah is named after African grasslands where its close relative, the serval cat, is to be found, which also helped to lay the foundations for the breed: the first and subsequent generations derived from the breeding of a serval to a domestic Bengal cat. The International Progressive Cat Breeders' Alliance (IPCBA) was the first international all-breed registry to recognize Savannahs for registration. The goal of the Savannah breeding program was to create a domestic cat which has physical features that link it with the serval, but combined with the loving, dependable temperament of the typical domestic cat.

The Savannah has a large, muscular build, a long neck and large, round ears, with distinctive black 'tear drop' markings on the eyes.

The Savannah has a reasonably docile temperament. They make great family pets and are easy to care for. They are loyal, intelligent, and have an outgoing personality. They make excellent companions for children as well as other pets.

The sleek coat is spotted, striped, or marbled. Colors include: Amber, Silver, Solid Black, and Black Smoke.

SCOTTISH FOLD

In 1961 a Scottish shepherd noticed a cat with strangely folded ears. This cat, called Susie, was the founder of the breed to which all of today's Scottish Folds are related. A breeding program was begun in the UK, but it was discovered that the dominant gene that caused the folded ears could also cause skeletal problems. The GCCF, among others, resisted recognition of the breed, and the main center of activity for the breed switched to the USA. Today's Scottish Fold cats were developed originally by outcrossings to British Shorthairs and to American Shorthairs in the USA. They now resemble these cats in type, aside from the shape of their

ears. Those with normal ears, often described as Scottish Straightears, are mated with cats which have folded ears to avoid genetic problems.

The Scottish Fold has a round face with wide round eyes and the ears folding tightly forward over the head. The ears should be small with rounded tips. The body is compact with a short neck. The tail is medium to long, flexible, and tapering.

The short, soft, dense coat is kept in good condition with the minimum of brushing and combing. The folded ears should be gently cleaned inside the folds with a damp cotton bud.

Colors include: White, Black, Blue, Red, Cream, Tortoiseshell, Calico, Dilute Calico, Blue-cream, Chinchilla, Shaded Silver, Shell Cameo, Black Smoke, Blue Smoke, Cameo Smoke, and Bi-color. Classic and Mackerel

Tabby in Brown, Blue, Red, Cream, Cameo, and Silver. Patched Tabby in Brown, Blue, and Silver. There are both short- and long-coated versions of this breed, differing only in terms of their coat length.

A loving, placid and companionable cat that loves both humans and other pets. These cats can cope with cold, harsh weather and have the farm cat's resistance to disease. Many Scottish Folds have the habit of sitting upright and tapping their owner with a paw. They often sleep on their backs with their legs in the air.

TO MRS. RENOLDS'S CAT

John Keats (1795-1821)

Cat! who has pass'd thy grand climacteric,
How many mice and rats hast in thy days
Destroy'd? How many tit-bits stolen? Gaze
With those bright languid segments green, and prick
Those velvet ears – but prithee do not stick
Thy latent talons in me, – and up-raise
thy gentle mew, and tell me all thy frays,
Of fish and mice, and rats and tender chick;
Nay, look not down, nor lick thy dainty wrists, –
For all the wheezy asthma - and for all
Thy tail's tip is nick'd off, and though the fists
Of many a maid have given thee many a maul,
Still is thy fur as soft as when the lists
In youth thou enter'dst on glass-bottled wall.

SELKIRK REX

This naturally curly cat originated from a stray blue-cream and white non-pedigree kitten found in Wyoming, USA in 1987. She was given to a Persian breeder who bred her to a black Persian.
She produced three curly

kittens out of six, proving that, unlike the Cornish and Devon Rexes (pages 140–147), the mother's mutation was dominant. Because of this, curly kittens can be born in the same litter as straight-haired kittens. Several more breedings proved that she carried the genes for both point restriction and long hair. Because of this, the decision was made to allow all colors and both hair lengths in the breed.

A medium to large cat with heavy bones that give the cat surprising weight and an impression of power, which is a direct reflection of its Persian ancestry. The head is rounded with wide cheeks. The eyes are round, full, and wide-set. Ears are medium and pointed. The legs are medium and the paws large. The tail is thick and tapers to a slightly rounded tip.

The cat has a random, unstructured coat, arranged in loose, individual curls. The curls appear in 'clumps' rather than as an overall wave. Maintaining the curl and coat is the same as for a longhaired cat, while combing and brushing before bathing is necessary. All the hairs are present, but curled, including the whiskers.

These are extremely patient, loving, and tolerant cats with an endearing personality. There are not many of these available as pets because most curly cats, especially females, are in breeding programs. Males are usually more readily available and make wonderful, affectionate pets. Both longhaired and shorthaired versions are possible.

"It is a very inconvenient habit of kittens (Alice had once made the remark) that, whatever you say to them, they always purr."

Lewis Carroll (1832-1898)

SIAMESE

With its distinctive looks, the Siamese is one of the world's most instantly recognizable breeds. It originated in Asia more than 500 years ago, where it held special status as guardian of the royal temples of Siam (now Thailand), and was revered by monks and royalty alike. In the late 1800s, the first breeding pair were brought to the UK. These were stockier cats with rounder heads than would become the fashion in later years. The popularity of the Siamese peaked around the 1950s. Since then, there has been a decline in their appeal attributed by some to a move towards a more

A Blue Point.

OPPOSITE: A Seal Point kitten.

extremely elongated, angular look. Recently, there has been a resurgence of interest in a more traditional 'applehead' look (see Traditional Siamese Cat, page 218).

A Tabby Point OPPOSITE: A Seal and a Chocolate Point.

These tall and graceful cats have a svelte build, long, slim legs, and a long head. They are also fine-boned with taut muscles. Face-on, the head from the tip of the ears to the muzzle forms a pronounced wedge shape. The eyes are almond-shaped and slanted, and a brilliant clear blue. The ears are very prominent and pointed. The paws are dainty and oval, while the tail is very long, thin at the base and tapering to a fine point.

The Siamese has a very short, fine coat that is glossy, silky and close-lying. Grooming is easy but must be done regularly. Young cats are pale at birth and the coloration of their points only emerges gradually.

Pointed colors include: Seal, Blue, Chocolate, Lilac, Cinnamon, Caramel, Fawn, Red, Cream, and Apricot. Tortie point: Seal, Blue, Chocolate, Lilac, Cinnamon, Caramel, and Fawn. Tabby point: Seal, Blue, Chocolate, Lilac, Red, Cream, Cinnamon, Caramel, Fawn, and Apricot. Torbie point: Seal, Blue, Chocolate, Lilac, Cinnamon, Caramel, and Fawn.

A lively and playful cat, the Siamese is loyal and affectionate but can be aloof. These cats are famed for their loud voices and big personalities. They make better pets when kept in pairs or small groups. Few cats are more ready to climb, both outdoors and in the home. Since Siamese become sexually mature very early in life – sometimes when just four months old, although six months is more usual – be prepared to arrange for young queens in particular to be neutered at the appropriate stage, to prevent unwanted kittens.

An Apricot Point.

OPPOSITE: A Chocolate Tabby Point.

TRADITIONAL SIAMESE
(Applehead)

Traditional Siamese (also known as Appleheads due to their head-shape) are the original cats of the royal family of Siam (now Thailand). These cats were used to guard the temples probably as far back as the 14th century. Appleheads were introduced into Europe towards the end of the 19th century. In recent years, the standard in cat shows for the Siamese breed is to have a stylized, very elongated wedge-shaped head – far removed from the more rounded head of the original Siamese. The Applehead is no longer acknowledged as being Siamese and, therefore, not professionally shown, apart from at traditional cat shows. CFA-Registered Traditional Siamese have become extremely rare.

Currently, the Applehead is enjoying something of a revival as cat owners favor a return to the traditional, round-headed look. This has, in part, been driven by fears of health problems ensuing from the very exaggerated, elongated head-shape that found favor in the 1950s.

A round face and muscular body. Distinctive blue eyes.

Pointed colors include: Blue, Chocolate, Lilac, and Seal.

The temperament is relatively calm and generally considered to be less frenetic than the modern Siamese. Applehead cats are agile, demonstrative, graceful, loyal, affectionate, devoted, intelligent, and resourceful. However, they can be domineering, and they are very vocal.

SINGAPURA

During the 1970s, an American cat breeder found a colony of unusual-looking feral cats in Singapore. They were known as 'drain cats,' and at one time were culled by the Singaporeans. The cats were first taken to the USA in 1975 and all registered Singapuras today originate from this breeding program. The name 'Singapura' is Malaysian for Singapore.

Ranked as one of the smallest breeds in the world, typically weighing less than 6 pounds (2.7kg), the Singapura is nevertheless stocky and muscular in build. Its head is round, its ears large and its eyes are huge, almond-shaped, and colored brilliant hazel, green or yellow. The nose and eyes are accentuated by

dark eye-liner-like outlines. The tail is slightly shorter than the body and slender with a blunt tip.

The fine, short, close-lying coat is in a ticked tabby with some markings on the backs of the legs, but not on the front. Each hair should have at least two bands of dark ticking separated by light bands of color. Each individual hair is light next to the skin and dark at the tip. The Singapura is one of the few breeds that is only available in one color, called sepia agouti. It is a warm ivory overlaid with sepia-brown, with paler underparts. Grooming is very easy. A light combing removes dead hairs, and occasional brushing tones the skin. Hand-grooming or stroking with a silk scarf imparts a healthy-looking sheen to the coat.

The Singapura is affectionate, good-natured, extremely gentle, and playful. Unfortunately, it is still not widely available and ranks among the more costly breeds.

SNOWSHOE

The result of a cross between Siamese and American Shorthairs, the Snowshoe originated in the USA in the 1960s. The breed remained little known until the 1980s, since when it has gained in popularity but still remains quite rare. Snowshoes faced opposition from Siamese breeders who feared that its characteristic white feet markings could become widely distributed in Siamese bloodlines if cross-breeding took place; but this fear has proved to be groundless.

With the distinctive white feet that gave rise to its name, the Snowshoe retains the dark points of the Siamese on its legs, tail, face, and ears. Its eye color is a bright, sparkling blue. The Snowshoe's muscular body is medium to large with medium legs and a medium to large tail. The head is

triangular, with large almond-shaped eyes that are slightly slanted and large, pointed ears. As in the case of other large breeds, toms tend to be significantly heavier than queens.

The short to medium, fine, glossy, close-lying coat needs the minimum of grooming with regular gentle brushing.

Colors include Seal Point and Blue Point. The Snowshoe is highly gregarious and will follow family members about the house. It hates to be alone and needs a good deal of companionship and attention. Its soft, delicate voice reveals its affectionate nature.

SPHYNX

The modern Sphynx breeding program began in 1966 in Toronto, Canada, when an ordinary shorthaired, black-and-white domestic cat gave birth to a hairless male kitten. The breed was developed from mother and son. Subsequently, crosses with Devon rexes have been used to expand the breed's bloodline. The Sphynx is not popular with many cat fanciers, however, and is not widely recognized for show purposes because of health worries resulting from the absence of its coat. This is a breed essentially suited to indoor living, away from the vagaries of the weather. The lack of fur makes these cats vulnerable to the cold, while exposure to hot sun can lead to sunburn, particularly over largely unpigmented areas of skin.

The Sphynx is a well-built, sturdy cat with a head slightly longer than it is wide, set on a long, slender neck. The large, wide-open ears are tall

and the outer edge is in line with the wedge of the face. Cheekbones are prominent and there are few or no whiskers. It has long, slim legs with elegant rounded paws and long toes. The tail is long and finely tapered. All

colors and patterns are acceptable. Colors in the Sphynx are often warmer than they are in cats with coats, because the natural pink of the skin is able to show through.

A lively, playful and mischievous cat, the Sphynx is very people-oriented, but does not like being held or petted. They are not keen on other cats.

The suede-like, wrinkled skin is covered with a soft, warm down, like the skin of a peach. There may be visible fur on the brow, around the toes, and at the tip of the tail. The skin needs daily cleaning, as the cat's empty hair follicles have oil-producing glands that cause it to sweat. People normally allergic to cats may find they can tolerate the furless Sphynx.

TEACUP CAT

It is said that Teacup cats originated from South America where they were found surviving in a back alley. They were caught and brought to Canada where they were bred successfully.

A Teacup cat is a small breed of cat. However, they possess all the attributes of their larger cousins.

Due to their small size it seems that it is impractical to home them before 5 months old, otherwise they are normal healthy kittens.

A good breeder will limit the number of litters to ensure that the queen stays healthy. This will help to ensure the gene pool is kept wide. Inbreeding should be avoided as offspring born from a diverse gene pool are more likely to experience good health.

Teacup cats are very small, miniature cats and are smaller than the usual category of miniature cats. Miniature cats are usually about one third to one half the size of normal size cats of the same breed. As a guideline teacup females weigh 2-4 pounds (0.90-1.90 kg) while the males are 3-6 lbs (1.36-2.70 kg).

They are generally less than 9 inches tall or less when adult. Teacup kittens are more vulnerable than normal sized kittens. Being miniature can pose certain problems so they are relatively high maintenance.

They are popular with those who may live in a small house or apartment or may just like the idea of owning a small, kitten-like cat.

Teacup cats are most commonly Persian in origin with long coats, and display the usual Persian colors.

TONKINESE

The Tonkinese displays the physical features of its mixed parentage – the product of a mating between a Siamese and a Burmese in the USA in the 1950s. The Tonkinese has the points of the Siamese, but with a softer-lined body, less angular head and quieter nature. Such mixed parentage means that the matings of two Tonkinese will not produce an all-Tonkinese litter. The result is most likely to be two Tonkinese to one each of Siamese and Burmese.

The Tonkinese is of medium build, with a wedge-shaped head with high cheekbones and strong contours to the brow, cheek and profile. The chin is firm and the eyes almond-shaped and slanted. The eye color is blue-green or turquoise. The ears have oval tips and the hair on them is very short. The legs are slim

and the paws oval. The tail is medium to long and tapers.

The coat is short, close-lying, fine and soft, with a lustrous sheen. The pattern shades to a darker tone on the legs, ears, mask and tail. The coat color is paler than the Burmese but darker than the Siamese. It is easy to keep in good condition with very little grooming.

Colors include: Brown Point, Chocolate Point, Blue Point, Red Point, and Lilac Point.

The Tonkinese has all the lively curiosity and affection of an Oriental breed, but without the loud insistent personality. It is a good choice for a person new to cats and is also suitable for families with children. It is an easy cat to train. Tonkinese cats love the outdoor life and should not be confined to a small flat or left alone for hours on end.

NON-PEDIGREE CATS

Of the 100 million or more pet cats worldwide, non-pedigrees (or random-bred or 'mixed-bred)', if you prefer) vastly outnumber pedigree cats. Up until the end of the 1800s, people mostly kept cats in order to keep down the vermin in their houses and barns. Only the rich kept cats for fun. It was with the introduction of specific breeding programs that the concept of the pedigree (and therefore non-pedigree) cat was born. While some people favor the looks, character traits, and habits of pedigree cats, a happy, healthy mixed-breed can be every bit as rewarding. Due to the endless possible combinations in their ancestry, a mixed-breed's appearance and character is, of course, unpredictable. However, a great many people feel it's worth taking the risk for the sake of a friendly companion.

Some non-pedigree cats closely resemble particular breeds. However, most have the moderate build that is typical of the British and American Shorthairs. Apart from color and coat, mixed-breeds differ much less from each other than pure breeds do, having not acquired the extremes of cobbiness or elongation that have been introduced into pedigree lines by selective breeding. Wedge-shaped heads and flattened faces are unusual in mixed-breeds but do sometimes appear if one of the parents includes a cat with Siamese or Persian genes in its recent history. Eyes are usually green or yellow and most non-pedigree cats have fairly long noses.

Because the gene determining short hair is dominant, most cross-bred cats are shorthaired, but there is no standard cross-bred type.

In general, non-pedigree cats are energetic, as this is nature's way of selecting the fittest and most successful animals. A distinct advantage of owning a mixed-breed is that they have much lower concentrations of undesirable genes and are therefore less prone to disability and disease. With proper care, a non-pedigree cat should live a long life. The typical mixed-breed, if you choose carefully, is a beautiful, intelligent, playful, low-maintenance companion with an independent streak.

Many mixed-breeds are tabbies, which is the variety closest to the cat's ancestor – the African wildcat, while bi-colors and tortoiseshells are also common. Solid colors are less common; however,

black, white, marmalade, and blue do occur, usually broken with traces of white fur, typically under the chin. White is common, both on its own and in combination with other solid and tabby colors.

INDEX